A Memoir of the South Western Circuit

GERARD A. LEE, S.C.

A Memoir of the South Western Circuit

WITH A FOREWORD BY

**The Honourable
Mr Justice Gerard Lardner**

Moytura Press • Dublin

The typesetting of this book was
produced by Gilbert Gough Typesetting for
Moytura Press, Ormond Court,.
11 Lower Ormond Quay, Dublin 1.

BRITISH LIBRARY CATALOGUING IN PUBLICATION DATA
Lee, Gerard A.
A memoir of the South Western Circuit.
1. Ireland (Republic). Barristers — Biographies
I. Title
344.1707

ISBN 1-871305-05-5

Printed in Ireland by
Betaprint Ltd

Contents

Acknowledgements

The author and the publisher would like to thank Con Healy, editor of the Limerick Association Yearbook, for permission to reproduce the chapters on Limerick and Kerry.

Preface

It was traditionally expected that barristers on circuit would stay at the same hotel and dine together in the evenings. In this way the integrity of the circuit unit was preserved and younger men enjoyed the company of their colleagues. A Bar-room was provided in each hotel where cases were prepared and legal knowledge was shared. It was a valuable training for young barristers in the practice of their craft. During the war years and for a considerable time later this communal life remained intact and hotel expenses remained reasonable.

With the coming of tourists, improved transport and high inflation, cracks began to appear on this monastic edifice. Bar-rooms were no longer provided in hotels and expenses for accommodation and meals greatly increased so that today many circuit court barristers live locally and attend the court sittings as required. Within the courthouse, however, the old traditions and procedures are still essentially the same as in the days of Cicero, O'Connell and Isaac Butt.

A benefit of this more liberal approach was

that one became acquainted with local people and more journeys were made beyond the environs of the circuit towns. Each summer Dermot Kinlen generously organised excursions to the Skelligs and a picnic lunch was provided by a Killarney hotel while Jack O'Shea and I frequently went to Glenbeigh for dinner when the judge had risen for the day.

On one occasion in court I mentioned to William Binchy that the guards who were present appeared to be very young. 'No', he said, 'they are about the same age as those who used formerly attend the sittings. The truth is that we are getting older ourselves'. Year by year the various categories of court officials and attendants began to look young and, when I discovered that the Pope in Rome was younger than myself, the time had come to collect the memories of a past generation and present them to the kindly reader lest they perish for ever within the tomb of oblivion.

Foreword

For some years Gerard Lee has ceased to be a regular attender at the Circuit Court sessions in the towns of the South Western Circuit. He may be an occasional visitor for special cases. His practice has been latterly as a silk in the High Court and the Supreme Court in Dublin and he has worked daily at his desk in the Law Library. It is nearly fifty years since he was called to the bar. It cannot have escaped his notice how greatly the Library has changed since he first began to attend here. The number of members of the bar has multiplied. The pre-eminent characters and personalities of those days are long departed. The ranks of old friends have become grievously thinned.

Some such considerations as these must, I think, have turned his thoughts back to his early years at the bar, but not, curiously, to life in the Law Library and the Courts in Dublin. His early and continuing affection has clearly been for the countryside and the towns of Limerick (his native county and the home of his forebears) and of Kerry and Clare. This slim volume is described as a memoir of the South Western Circuit in the years after 1942. For perhaps ten or fifteen years the Ireland of 1942, the life of the countryside and the Circuit towns with their courthouses and antiquated hotels, the way of life of the bar and of the solicitors which he describes, continued, not greatly changed from the early years of the century. There followed then a new era of great change in every aspect of life; so that the Ireland and the South Western Circuit of 1942 have become only a memory.

It is this memory which Gerard Lee recalls in prose which brings to life the woods and waters and hills of Kerry and Clare and of his beloved Limerick; the Circuit towns with their graceful stone courthouses and galleried courtrooms; the antiquated yet friendly hotels; the way of life and travel of the Circuit barristers. It is into his topographical descriptions that the author has most vividly breathed life. It also recalls with affection and appreciation many of the members of the bar and the Circuit Judges who travelled the Circuit in those days. I am not sure that, with one exception, they are realised or made so vividly alive to the reader as are the countryside and the towns and the life of the Circuit barrister. Perhaps this is because the good nature and the warm heart which the author possesses and which exclude all unkindness or malice, inhibit him from the sharply limned portrait. The one unconscious exception is the author himself. This memoir bears the clear imprint of his personality. It reveals a person apt for friendship, a lover of books and landscape, a man of civilised tastes and interests, someone who has been preserved from worldliness. Those who know him will recognise his individual voice coming through it's prose.

Reading this memoir has given me great pleasure. I hope it will be enjoyed by many others and that the Author may be moved to write a further and more adventurous volume

Gerard Lardner
The High Court

To the memory of
Maurice Danaher

The Circuit Court in Limerick

One afternoon in 1940, when we sat for the autumn degree examination in Earlsfort Terrace, a great noise filled the room as a black German warplane flew past the window with a British fighter plane in pursuit. The noise gradually faded into the quietness of the day and we proceeded with our Roman Law paper. The years which followed were among the saddest in history as the war swelled like an angry sea and destroyed traditional populations and ancient places alike without mercy. In another event of great sadness the nations of Eastern Europe were abandoned and they had now become lost to us perhaps forever. This was the background that greeted my early years in the Circuit Court in Limerick. Having been called to the Bar in June 1942 I attended the court without delay and the memories of those days have always remained fresh.

The barristers stayed at Cruise's Hotel where their predecessors had stopped since the 18th century. It was still the 'old Cruise's before the renovation of later years. One entered through the great doorway with its fan-light and side

1

windows. The tiled hall led to the Georgian stair-case with its rickety balustrade and, beside the office, a blackboard was hanging on which one chalked the hour of the morning call. In the rooms were wooden beds and dressing tables with moveable mirrors and plenty of drawers. The faded paper was often peeling from the walls while the sagging floors and noisy old windows radiated an atmosphere of the past. Sometimes, when the moonlight poured in through the great windows in the back rooms, bringing into relief the outline of a tall wardrobe or an antique fireplace and anointing the whole room with the oil of serenity, a timeless picture emerged which would have delighted the Impressionists of earlier years.

The dining-room was still in its original form with its ceiling and cornice intact and the warm satin-like paper on the walls. We usually occupied the three tables near the windows which looked out towards the Victorian facade of Cannock's and the big mechanical clock. There, in comfortable mahogany chairs, we all sat down to dinner. The communal side of the Circuit was still intact and the circumstances of those years did nothing to destroy this aspect of Circuit life.

Although the amount of work was limited, food and accommodation were cheap. During my first year the daily rate in the hotel was increased, by one shilling, to fourteen shilling and six pence. It was the thin end of the wedge and what a wedge

2

it proved to be! This tariff included bed and breakfast and a full lunch and dinner. In addition a room on the first floor was provided as a Bar-room. There we prepared our cases and read the papers while, around the fire intellectual conversations and arguments often took place. This room was no. 20 with its tall windows and faded prints of English cathedrals, its smoky atmosphere and the turf fire that never seemed to die.

Eventually there were only two trains each week from Dublin as the war progressed. These journeys, in over-crowded wooden carriages with side corridors and steam engines driven on turf and slack-briquettes, were a real test of endurance when compared with travel by inter-city or super trains of today. An improvement came when some all-steel carriages were introduced and these were greatly prized by seasoned travellers. Later two large green steam engines — the Maeve and the Macha — were purchased as coal again became readily available. Then came the change to diesel and the passing of the smuts and sparks associated with steam.

I remember seeing the hedges brown and burnt from the sparks of passing trains during heat waves and, occasionally, cocks of hay were destroyed. The departure of steam and the nostalgic whistle of the train meant the passing of a romantic age in transport. When the super trains were introduced a degree of prosperity was commencing for barristers and we often travelled first class with meals served in the carriage. This was luxury indeed when compared with wartime travel although the seats were never as comfortable or dignified as in the old first-class carriages of long ago.

During those constant journeys one became used to the changing character of the landscape and its varying colours season by season. The approaching towns became associated with the spires and towers of passing churches or the presence of a rural landmark of forest, parkland or distant hills. In an exceptional spring one discovered the profusion of blackthorn blossoms on the fences and gorse in the glens and on the high slopes. And, with the commencement of a warm summer, the hawthorn and elder were often so brilliant that it appeared as though snow had fallen but had lodged only on the hedges.

Occasionally, as evening approached, the sky became a complex of colours as the sun adorned the surface of clouds with delicate shades of red and pink and with a background of the lightest blue or gray. I remember, during beautiful days in April, watching the sun sinking behind the Devil's Bit mountain near Templemore like a great red dome disappearing behind the hill. The scene was repeated in other April days and I have rarely seen the evening sky so majestic as in that short but splendid period of spring.

My first brief was from Roger Fox a well-known solicitor from Kilmallock. It was an application relating to the sale of land in a judgment-mortgage suit. Judge O'Donnell granted the order and said that, as I was instructed by a very experienced solicitor, he was sure that the proofs were correct. Afterwards he told me that it was difficult to establish a practice on the Circuit but that I had good friends among the solicitors. And so it proved to be in County Limerick as well as in Kerry and Clare. The city of Limerick, however, remained distant.

In those years the courthouse was in a rather dilapidated condition but it has long since been restored. Only one of the two courtrooms was then in use the other being occupied as a store for papers, boxes and various articles of furniture. In the middle stood the dock which was topped with iron spikes. The central seats of pitch-pine were curved in a semi-circle towards the bench and this made it a pleasant and comfortable place in which to work. Behind the dock were the seats for witnesses and the public. The Bar-room, which was on the first floor, was reached by a flight of broad and gradual stairs in period style. It had formerly been used by the grand jury and a map of County Limerick and its baronies hung from the wall. It was a long and graceful room with a huge old fireplace and several large windows. It is now used for offices.

The view from that room had a special charm with the crumbling remains of Arthur's Quay and the old corn store, the boat club and the bridge and the great river in all its moods and forms bedecked with swans and boats and bobbing buoys. O Limerick ! how I have loved your ancient places — the warehouses and markets, churches and bridges, buildings of brick and limestone in the quiet of a summer evening and the little squares and convents hidden away behind their own protective walls. Above all I loved the river at full tide as it journeyed slowly towards the setting sun. Then, Limerick, you were a lady content for ever within your princedom by the sea.

Certain types of cases came frequently before the court as a result of the war. Ejectment cases were common and they were often decided on the question of where the greater hardship lay. Due to the shortage of coal, timber and turf which constituted the principal source of heat, the trees on boundary fences became valuable. In East Limerick many double fences existed between farms. Academic discussion often took place as to the origin of these wide boundaries and it was generally considered that they either represented the line between landlords' estates or were constructed as roads or passages to facilitate internal communication in an area where the land was rich and the soil deep and difficult to cross in wet weather. Trees were frequently planted on top, or at the edge, of fences and they were now mature and needed for fuel. If there

6

was clear evidence of a drain at each side then, in the absence of more positive proof, it was considered that the fence was owned jointly. If there was a drain at one side only the farmer on the other side was considered to be the owner of the whole fence and, of course, the trees also as it was assumed that his predecessor had originally gone to the end of his land and then erected the fence on his own field with soil taken from the area of the drain.

An interesting case of this kind was heard in 1943 in which John Ryan of Scarteen was the plaintiff. His neighbour claimed joint ownership of trees on a wide bank which had a drain at each side. In default of positive evidence to the contrary the trees would be owned jointly. However the plaintiff produced an old parchment document signed by the Clerk of the Crown and Peace to the effect that the plaintiff's ancestor had planted the bank with trees about one hundred years earlier and, by virtue of an 18th century Irish statute enacted to encourage the planting of timber trees, he would be entitled to their ownership at the end of his tenancy. Evidence was also given that the trees in dispute were of a certain species and age so as to identify them with the trees in the certificate. The plaintiff succeeded in his claim. Several rather similar cases came before the court in those years.

Cases relating to easements of rights of way and the right to water cattle at a stream were relatively common although these were more frequent in Kerry and Clare than in County Limerick. Claims for compensation for malicious damage to property appeared in the lists but were much less numerous than later while cases under the Workmen's Compensation Acts constituted a considerable amount of the litigation. Claims arising out of cattle trespass, breach of contract, breach of warranty in the sale of turf and negligence and nuisance cases were common. Some days were set aside for criminal jury trials and district court appeals, and part of a day was allotted to equity cases which usually related to administration and mortgagee matters.

In my first criminal case I appeared for the accused who was charged with having had unlawful carnal knowledge of a girl under the age of seventeen years. The defendant pleaded guilty and an application for leniency was made to the court on the grounds that the defendant and the girl wished to marry and the girl's parents were agreeable. Counsel for the State objected on the grounds that the accused was already married and that a record of the marriage existed. Some years previously the parents of another girl had forced the defendant to go through a form of marriage with her in the home of an elderly parish priest. The parties never lived together afterwards. An adjournment was then obtained in the trial to enable the accused to make an application to the ecclesiastical court to have his 'marriage' condemned. Two diocesan courts found that the marriage took place because of grave unjust fear and that it was not binding. The defendant was not required to proceed to the Sacred Rota in Rome. When the case again came before Judge O'Briain he imposed a suspensory sentence of six months imprisonment.

Some years earlier a rather similar case was heard by Judge McElligott in Limerick. The accused was a young man with flaming red hair. Having heard the evidence the judge adjourned the passing of sentence until the end of the day. At four o'clock the defendant appeared again in the dock in fear and trembling. The judge looked at the unfortunate prisoner with his usual sternness and said 'Now my red-haired Romeo I am going to deal with you. I will imprison you until the rising of the court. The court will now rise'. Another story from Judge McElligott's court concerned a West Limerick farmer who had employed a contractor to erect an outside lavatory on his farm. When the work was completed the farmer refused to pay the price and litigation ensued. At the court the amount was agreed between the parties subject to the defendant's liability. Before rising for the day counsel prevailed on the reluctant judge to hear the defendant briefly as the issue between the parties was now clear-cut. When asked why he refused to pay for the work the farmer turned to the judge and said: 'I refuse to pay a penny my Lord, because the building he erected was so narrow that you had to untackle outside and then back into it'!

In jury actions one learned at an early stage that the members of the jury were not officers of the court. They were in the nature of guests who had been invited to adjudicate on the facts and they should be treated accordingly. One learned also that a speech to the jury should, as far a possible, adhere to the ideals of sincerity, clarity and brevity.

Occasionally we walked around the bridges after dinner or went to Corbally or along the embankment. I frequently stayed with relations in the country and sometimes had a walk in the Greenwood or on Blackrock mountain near Glenosheen and visited remote Abbey cemetery, among the hills, where my forebears lie at rest.

Life on the circuit, however, was not always so relaxed. Tensions frequently arose and were associated with scarity of work, legal problems, adjournments of cases, the collection of fees and, sometimes, temperamental differences among colleagues and one's relationship with the Bench. 'Know the facts and the law will look after itself' was the wise advice from an experienced colleague and he could have added that it was better to know your judge than to know the law. New legal principles were rarely decided in the Circuit Court; there were no juries in civil cases and the essential elements in most actions were the presentation of relevant evidence and the handling of witnesses. Life on the Circuit was quite difficult and demanding. It required dedication but, if the art of living is the art of movement, then there was a certain amount of that in the life of a Circuit barrister. When bitten by the bug it was difficult to change.

Once each term we went to Rathkeale for a day, leaving Cruise's at nine o'clock. It was a welcome diversion because we passed through the beautiful countryside around Adare and spent the day away from the city. William Binchy used to remark that all the cases in Rathkeale were agricultural ones. He was right. Grazing and agistment, trespass, breaches of warranty, easements and District Court appeals formed the bulk of the business.

The courthouse, set in a little square, was archaic and formed a perfect setting for such cases. In front was a double flight of steps and over the portal was an ancient clock similar to ones which may be seen in continental towns. Inside it had the old-fashioned arrangement of seats with the barristers and solicitors facing each other near the judge and the witness seated in the central platform. From one side the parkland and trees of a country house could be seen through a side window and, from the adjoining room, one had a view of the low range of hills near the town and the yard at the back where, Maurice Danaher said, some of the insurgents of 1798 were executed.

After one o'clock we adjourned for lunch to Johnson's emporium which was an old-fashioned shop with the statue of a Chinaman over the door and, inside, was a great assortment of goods behind the pitch-pine counter. The floor was paved with well-worn round cobblestones. In an adjoining room we had a light lunch of cold meat and tea, a special feature being slices of Swiss roll and a large jug of cream. I will always remember with affection that day in Rathkeale as I remember also with affection the day each term on which we went to Kilrush which had a courthouse as archaic and an atmosphere as memorable as those in Rathkeale.

During my years as a junior barrister four judges presided in the South Western Circuit. Thomas O'Donnell, who had been an M.P. for West Kerry with the Irish Party, was in office for a few years only. A kind and courteous man he welcomed me on my first appearence and he died in 1943. Barra O'Briain was appointed in 1943 and, apart from a few years, when he was a judge in Cyprus, he remained until his retirement in 1973. Eventually he was appointed president of the Circuit Court. While the volume of work was not extensive during his period in office nevertheless legal arguments were welcomed and legal judgments were frequent. As a fluent Irish speaker he encouraged the use of the native language in his court. Formality was preserved during cases but there were occasions when the atmosphere became rather strained. While the proceedings moved slowly his charges to the jury in criminal cases were, however, thorough and elegant.

He was followed by Herbert Wellwood whose most endearing trait was the quality of his mercy. He was not a jurist but a poor litigant or the accused in a criminal trial always received fair and compassionate treatment. On his retirement in 1977 Timothy Desmond became judge. During his term of office the volume of work increased greatly. He completed the lists with expedition and, while his judgments were few, his decisions were numerous. And they were mainly decisions on the facts of cases.

With changes in the social and economic conditions changes have also occurred in the courts. To a considerable extent the character of the litigation has altered with the passing of new legislation and the big increase in crime and personal injury cases. There is a tendency to specialise professionally and the modern young barrister tends to be more of a executive rather than a contemplative. These gradual changes in the character of the Bar resemble the course of a river which is frequently forced to alter direction on its journey to the sea. Nevertheless it remains the same river. *Plus ça change, plus c'est la même chose*.

Among my deceased colleagues five stand out clearly in my memory. These are Maurice

Danaher, George Kenny, Maurice Fitzgerald, Tom Pigot and William Binchy.

Maurice Danaher was a native of Athea and had spent some years lecturing in economics in Hong Kong and Peking. His knowledge was truly astonishing and he was a friend of all lawyers who sought advice on points of law, pleadings or conveyancing. His essential intellectual trait was his broad culture and learning.

In literature and natural history, in topography and in the knowledge of ancient peoples he took a keen delight. He was a classical man but was also a very private person. Deeply shy and sensitive he adopted an almost oriental detachment and courtesy as a structure whereby to cloak that shyness and give it form. A lover of Latin Europe he particularly admired France as the chief intellectual exponent of that culture and he read French literature deeply in the orginal. A delightful trait of his was the discovery, for those who showed an interest, of half-neglected authors of great merit such as W.H. Hudson, A.Russel Wallace and many others in the literature of remote travel.

George Kenny's father had been a barrister on the Old Munster Circuit and later he became a Circuit Court judge in Cork. A lightly-built man with a moustache George was old-world in appearance and ways. While he never read as deeply as Maurice he used often sit on the brass fender in room 20 and read extracts from *The*

Times and the *Clare Champion* for our benefit or take his afternoon tea at the table as a solace before dinner. Few barristers knew their own people as well as George knew the people of Clare where he lived. In whatever court he was pleading he was an able advocate with a sharpness in cross-examination and a nimbleness of wit which were almost unique.

Maurice Fitzgerald lived in Limerick but we had the benefit of his company in court and sometimes in the hotel. Always friendly and loyal he was an intelligent man but not strictly an intellectual and, when the occasion required it, he was a fascinating talker and raconteur.

Tom Pigot came from one of the most traditional legal families in Ireland. His great grand father was Chief Baron Pigot who, as a young barrister, had assisted Daniel O'Connell in the Doneraile conspiracy trial in Cork. *His* son was David Richard who became Master of the Court of Exchequer. Tom Pigot's father was John H. who became a Circuit Court judge after 1924. Tom was one of the most refreshing of colleagues, completely free from snobbery or pretence and he was an excellent walker and talker. A fine speaker in court where he practised for some years, and then accepted an international post in the East.

William Binchy would rank with Maurice as another of the intellectually cultivated men at the bar. A native of Charleville he was equally learned in law, history and literature. He appeared to have read almost all the classics and was keeping Proust for later years as he felt that, if he read Proust's great novel, he would have few new pastures left. Once when I was reading a Russian novel in room 20 he expressed his approval but advised me to keep it in my room as solicitors were pragmatic people and expected barristers to be practical at least when on Circuit. He recalled the occasion when he had been reading *Finnegans Wake* in the Bar-room and had just closed it and was continuing with his work. At that moment a solicitor entered the room, opened the book and, after a few moments, placed it again on the table and said: 'Binchy, if I knew the barrister who was reading that book I would never give him a brief'! Eventually William had the biggest junior practice on the Circuit. His legal knowledge was fully appreciated by the court and his legal precedents, drafted in pure classical English, were eagerly sought and copied by younger colleagues.

One of the joys of the Circuit was in being present when Maurice and William discussed literature or history, the problems of law or life or the excitement of social gossip. Dare I say it but we shall not see their like again! They had a learning and European culture which was acquired in more leisurely days and which, in less than a generation, has become a luxury as we proceed down the skating-rink of modern life.

Many of the barristers live locally today as they do in Cork and elsewhere because more work is now being dealt with in the Circuit Courts and the cost of hotels has become excessive. As in many other cities and larger towns High Court jury trials in civil actions take place a few times each year in Limerick and most of the senior counsel who attend stay in the modern hotels on the outskirts. One would not find any ghosts from the past in Cruise's hotel today. The O'Connell room is the name appropiately given to the former No.20 and it is now used mainly as a show place for clothes and shoes.

The only echo of former days is likely to be the sound of my own foot-steps when I walk down the corridor as the last of the Circuit in a hotel which had formerly catered for the Munster Bar since the 18th century. And, as the shadows lengthen and evening approaches, the mind returns home from its wanderings having discovered that everything passes and everything fades away except memory.

The Circuit Court in Kerry

It was on the platform at Mallow station in 1943 that I first met Eoin O'Mahony. Both of us were waiting for the train to Tralee and, as I had my red-tasselled bag, he spoke to me and asked me if I was the new barrister in Kerry. During the journey he presented himself as a unique and colourful personality. He entertained the entire carriage with anecdotes that had a medieval flavour and with extracts from a recent sermon given by an Italian bishop. As Eoin was then unable to travel in Europe he usually came from Cork to the circuit court in Tralee and Killarney in order to meet his Kerry friends.

The barristers often brought food for the journey from Dublin although occasionally it was possible to get refreshments at a railway junction. Apart from conversation and reading certain parts of the landscape provided a real relief from the tedium of slow war-time travel. After Templemore the train descended into the rich valleys of Munster. The great forest of Dundrum was almost European in character and, eventually, the majestic appearance of the Galtees dominated the landscape.

No Irish hills are as serene or beautiful as these Tipperary mountains. At all times they appear as a unit of near-perfection varying frequently in mood but always constant in the loveliness of their form. I have seen them on summer days when the sun caught the light green shades of the slopes and isolated the deep furrows made by ancient streams as they tumbled downwards through the glens. Sometimes a stormy sky turned the mountains into a dark and angry mass and often they acquired a silver-gray sheen like satin which changed sensitively under the shadows or when clouds caressed the peaks for a while as they floated slowly across the sky in this green and misty island. During a severe winter the contrast of mountain and valley was reversed. The earth itself had now gone to sleep and the trees and fields were dull and windswept. It was then that the mountains appeared alive and dramatic when they were crowned by a sparkling white or by rose-pink colours of sunset on the snow.

Soon the train passed near the picturesque range of the Ballyhoura hills which rise in a semi-circular nest-like group in the quiet south eastern corner of County Limerick and separate from the plains of Cork. In that land are some of the most historic and evocative place-names in Munster: Ardpatrick, Glenosheen, Glenanaar, Seefin and Slieve Reagh and the towns of Buttevant, Doneraile and Kildorrery, the old medieval capital of Kilmallock and the little hill-town of Kilfinane which is almost enclosed by the wooded slopes where they blend gently with the fertile fields of the Golden Vein.

After Mallow the train for Kerry branched westwards along the Blackwater valley and, having passed through Banteer, with its own branch line for Kanturk and Newmarket, it journeyed through rich unspoiled farm land beside the green hills above Millstreet and into the border country of Slieve Luachra for ever hallowed as the heartland of the finest eighteenth century Gaelic poets and poetry of Munster. The streams then became more numerous and so did the winding mountain roads and little stone bridges as we approached the upper reaches of the Flesk and, leaving the Paps of Dana and Stoompa mountain on our left, the train glided quietly downwards beside the river and into the attractive station at Killarney before making the last lap of the journey home.

Tralee was one of the most popular towns on the circuit. The Grand Hotel in Denny Street where we stopped was a comfortable early Victorian building with ample accommodation, a Bar-room and better food than in the much-advertised luxury hotels of today. Every place in the town was convenient as the courthouse, the station and solicitors' offices were nearby. At the end of the street was the County Hall which was built of old red sandstone and a spacious town park which had formerly been part of the Denny estate. Beyond it was the road to Blennerville and Dingle.

As one walked down Denny Street the undulating folds of the Slieve Mish mountains, purple in their garment of heather, were visible from Scota's grave to Caherconree and Baurtrigoum where they reached down to the sea near Derrymore. The little river Lee rose to the east and, having acquired some tributaries along the way, flowed under the town and Musgrave bridge until it formed its own marshy estuary near Tralee bay. There it became a haven for sea birds whose plaintive cry one could frequently hear at night before entering into the land of Nod.

Sometimes we walked around the park with its fine beech and lime trees and flanked by elegant ecclesiastical buildings which were constructed from local sandstone. A more frequent walk was along the canal embankment from the town to Blennerville bridge beside the mountains and the estuary and then on to the point where the sea wall ended and the full glory of Tralee Bay was unfolded with the Magharee islands and the great bulk of Stradbally and Brandon mountains stretching into the sunset. An air of nostalgia hovered by the canal as the waters seeped in and out with the tide. No longer did it carry merchandise into the little harbour near the town and the only evidence of its former use was the hulk of an ancient barge which lay half buried in the mud and silt of the basin.

On the other side of the road were the tracks of the Tralee and Dingle light railway and I can recall seeing, during the war, one of the last of the goods trains puffing its way towards Dingle until it faded from sight under the shadow of the mountains. Over-all hung the silent melancholy of the sea with its vast desert of water lying for ever westwards.

Blennerville itself was a crumbling little residential village with a narrow old stone bridge, a 19th century windmill and half-slated houses of long ago. It was probably planned as a trading suburb of Tralee between the marshland and the bay and today it sleeps quietly as a relic of old decency from bygone days.

In those years the interior of the courthouse had a antique appearance. Two semi-circular courtrooms occupied the first floor and were surrounded by a circular stone corridor. The Bar-room, which was on the second floor, had windows that looked towards McCowen's busy flour mills and a convenient door provided a view into the centre of the court. A flight of stone steps led to the Bar-room and these had become worn thin at one side from the feet of generations of lawyers. The courtroom itself possessed a huge window high above the bench which provided sufficient light for the proceedings while, over the balcony, were some windows for ventilation but small enough for a prison cell.

The seats were curved in a semi-circle towards the bench and the witness stand which enabled every voice to be heard clearly. After years of indecision the interior has now been reconstructed in a different form. The alterations became necessary due to decay and the present arrangement was executed tastefully and with the happy addition of a central hall and consultation rooms. The magnificent exterior, consisting of a round temple of limestone with a long flight of steps and a double row of Ionic columns, has been retained and restored.

In Tralee we commenced work on Tuesday with criminal jury trials followed by district court criminal appeals. Sometimes 'white gloves' were presented to the judge by the county registrar as a token of the fact that the county was free from serious crime for those sittings. Eventually Judge O'Briain declined to accept gloves on such occasions because, with the increased jurisdiction of the district court in criminal matters, many relatively serious cases were now disposed of by that court under the new legislation. The jury trials which did proceed in the circuit court related mainly to larceny, embezzlement, fraudulent conversion, serious assaults and unlawful carnal knowledge.

From time to time a barrister is asked how he can justify defending a prisoner if he knows that the accused is guilty of the crime with which he is charged. One of the functions of defence counsel is to ensure as far as possible that the necessary proofs have been carried out by the State before a prisoner is found guilty. Furthermore, while counsel may have his suspicions in certain cases, he can never be certain that the accused is guilty unless the prisoner makes a confession of guilt to him. On one occasion I was asked to defend a prisoner who had been charged with stealing money from a book-maker's bag at Killarney races. A consultation was arranged in the cells at Tralee courthouse. The prisoner had an Irish name, he lived mainly in London and spoke with a Cockney accent. Eventually he turned to me and, raising his hands, said: 'Blyme guv'nor I ain't no saint. I done it alright'.

After a few moments I told him that he could get another counsel if he wished but that I was still free to defend him if he elected not to give evidence. He adopted the latter course. During the hearing the judge smiled broadly from time to time as the cross examination concentrated on the *minutiae* of the State proofs. A direction was refused and the jury returned a verdict of guilty. Evidence of previous convictions showed that the accused had stolen money from book-makers' bags at many well-known race meetings in England. He received a sentence of nine months imprisonment. My client was a professional thief but, as a person, he was likeable with considerable charm and bravado and a subtle sence of humour. He would not have been astray in one of the stories of Conan Doyle or Robert Louis Stevenson.

Other criminal cases from those years in Tralee were somewhat memorable because of the atmosphere created by the evidence. In one case where the accused was charged with obtaining money by threats of violence in the kitchen of a remote farm house much of the background of an old-fashioned Abbey Theatre play was present while in a case of assault and battery, in an overcrowded house in a poor area of Tralee, the sadness of Dostoevsky lingered heavily over the case. The most amusing criminal case in which I appeared in those early years was one in which the accused was charged with causing a public mischief which resulted in a waste of time for the gardai when they were required to investigate what turned out to be a hoax. It was the only case in the list that day and, as no brief for the accused had been handed out, the other barristers, who had come down early to breakfast, adjourned to the Bar-room to read the newspapers. Later, as I was finishing my meal, a solicitor from Killarney entered the room and, having greeted me in his usual hearty manner, said: 'First come, first served. The early bird catches the worm. Here is a brief in the public mischief case. There will be a plea of guilty and you will plead for leniency'!

The formal evidence disclosed that the accused

had reported a robbery from the mail van at Moll's Gap on the scenic mountain road between Killarney and Kenmare. Two gardai had then left Killarney on their bicycles and proceeded up the long climb to the scene of alleged crime only to find that the story was false. The accused was given a suspensory sentence.

On the civil side cases relating to turbary rights and rights of way, breach of contract, trespass, nuisance and negligence, breach of warranty and district court appeals formed a considerable part of the work while malicious injury applications and cases under the Workmen's Compensation Acts were the most frequent of the statutory claims.

My first brief in Kerry was from Edmond B. Slattery who was a well-known solicitor in Tralee. A certain lady had been travelling by train from Fieries on the Caherciveen line when she fell from the train at Molahiffe halt and suffered injuries. She had purchased a cheap market ticket that morning and the small print contained a term excluding the railway company from liability for negligence except where the injured person possessed a ticket at the standard rate. No settlement was offered to the plaintiff and, as there was a precedent for such a defence, my clients, who were the Great Southern Railway Company, had a technical victory. This protection for transport companies is not available today.

I can recall an interesting turary case which concerned the great bog near Lyracrumpane in North Kerry. It lasted for a full day in the circuit court and, on appeal it came before an elderly High Court judge in Tralee. The heavy atmosphere of the courthouse in humid weather was too much. Within half an hour the judge appeared to be asleep notwithstanding the deep resonant voice of John A. Costello S.C. who was on his feet. Counsel turned to his junior, William Binchy, and said: 'What will we do Bill? The judge is asleep.' 'Let him sleep', said William, 'we won in the court below and he can't reverse us'.

Shortly afterwards the opposing counsel, Kevin Liston S.C. rose to cross examine the witness and the change in timbre had a dramatic effect. The judge sat upright and said that it was a pity to see decent country people quarrelling about turf in Kerry and that an attempt should be made to settle the case. At noon negotiations commenced and, because a dozen people were interested personally in the outcome, the discussions and preparation of the settlement lasted until 4 p.m. when the consent was finally signed. Meanwhile the judge was confined to his room in which the only window was a skylight. On returning to the bench he said: 'Mr. Costello, I suggested that the parties should try to settle the case, but I did not anticipate that you would be engaged in drafting a peace treaty'.

The consent was indeed longer than many a

treaty as it was a document of several pages which involved much compromise before the final settlement was reached. Today it lies in the records of the court as an interesting local charter for Lyracrumpane.

Occasionally Eoin O'Mahony held a brief for the Kerry County Council in malicious injury applications and he appeared in an interesting case in Tralee relating to tolls and the poor rate. There the evidence established that a weekly market was held in premises in the town and charges were levied on persons who used the premises because in doing so they obtained facilities which included the use of a weigh-bridge, the housing of vehicles and stallage of animals. It was held that such charges did not constitute tolls for the purpose of liability to poor rate. The decision was cited later in a rather similar case in Cork in which it was likewise held that the fee charged to the public, when entering the grounds of Blarney Castle in order to enjoy the amenities, did not constitute a toll.

Tralee had plenty of interesting characters in those years. Ned Slattery had many amusing stories about his experiences. At one time he had been on a ranch in Argentina and, when asked what size it was, he said that a man would start to plough a furrow in the early morning and when he came to the end of the furrow it was time to lie down for the night! He was a charming and friendly gentleman of the old school and he gave me some kindly advice on my career. In his office was a clerk who was small in stature and Dickensian in appearance and manner. When instructing a barrister in a case he used to stand on a wooden butter box and look over his glasses as he pointed out the problems in the brief. Further up the street was Joe Guihan who was a typical family solicitor. He always looked dapper and had his hair brushed neatly across his head. On his attractive offices opposite the courthouse the words 'Law Chambers' were carved in stone over the door.

J.D. O'Connell, who was the county council solicitor, had the best law library in Tralee and, as the judge appreciated legal arguments, we were fortunate that his kindness permitted the use of these books in court. Briefs from the county council in malicious injury applications and workmen's compensation cases were distributed generously by Jeremiah Hickey, his junior solicitor. This distribution enabled some of us to survive during the difficult early years of a barrister's life on circuit. Kerry was always a friendly county where individual traits of character were respected and book learning was admired. As the towns were spread across the land rather evenly Kerry was essentially a rural county with the virtues of the countryside. Long may it remain so.

One of the 'characters' in the town was Mark O'Donnell who was proprietor of the Railway Bar in Ashe Street. He always kept some packets of cigarettes under the counter for us during the war and, on Sundays after Mass, the back room in his bar became an informal but exclusive club where some gentlemen of the parish met for drinks and conversation before returning home to dinner. The county registrar was Dan King who sat in court with a fine presence and eased the path of the judge on equity days. I remember him particularly on his great double-barred bicycle as he cycled down Denny Street to his home in Blennerville. I also remember Dr. Brick from Ballyheigue whose voice had become a whisper and who took you gently by the arm when telling you one of his stories, and Mr. Tuff the public engineer whose housing estate Maurice Danaher always admired because the hand of an artist was visible in the form and finish of the dwellings. I had great respect for these men who looked so wise and experienced. They had all been born well before the first World War and were reared by parents who were themselves mid-Victorians. They appeared to be quite old although they were only in late middle age but the people who were old when we were young were much older than the people who are old today!

After court consultations were often held in solicitors' offices and briefs were handed in to the hotel. We usually adjourned to the bar for a drink around the fire before dinner. During our meal and later in the Bar-room the talk on legal, social and historical topics was a real education and an aid towards the intellectual maturity of younger men. A genuine insecurity was, however, often present because of the relative scarcity of work and the tragedy of the war. In addition few of us had a private income at a time when the old financial and social standards were being shattered and fewer still knew where to turn for professional preferment. Our Circuit had its charms no less than it's difficulties but the days of the Old Munster Circuit had passed and the beautiful land of the south west had now become an inauspicious place from which to start one's climb to the woolsack. One colleague, whom I considered to be secure and mature, told me that at the Bar not only had one to keep going until one dropped but that his great fear was that he would die and leave his wife and children on the rates.

At that time the court sat in Listowel on Saturday and the following Monday. Sometimes we travelled as best we could to the town on Friday evening and put up at the Listowel Arms Hotel with its great turf fires and spacious old lounge and commerical room. It had a large central hall and winding stairs. In one of the bedrooms a picture over the fireplace showed a young boy holding a section of wool in both forearms while his grandmother was seated in an armchair and rolling the wool into a ball. At the open door were other boys with caps were shouting merry taunts at the unfortunate victim. Some of us went to Ballybunion on Saturday evening and stayed at the Central Hotel. We took a walk along the strand with a visit to the caves or a walk through the golf course to the river Cashen. In the hotel there was a fine set of photographs showing the Lartigue railway in the days of its glory.

One well-known case which appeared continually in the list was a complex administration suit with landlord and tenant overtones. At the back of the court a lone woman sat with her rosary beads and she prayed that her counsel would succeed in routing her rival with a *Jagoe v. Harrington* civil bill and a *Sweeney v. Sweeney* notice to quit ! It was also in Listowel that the judge fined a priest for refusing to give evidence relating to an interview between himself and two of his parishioners. The judge had applied the law as it was stated in the textbooks. On appeal Gavan Duffy J. held, in Tralee, that the refusal of the priest to give evidence was justified and was not a contempt of court because communications made in confidence to a parish priest in a private consultation were privileged.

Eventually we departed from Tralee on Saturday morning when travel became less difficult. William Binchy always left by the early Limerick train which he called the 'Dawn Express' through Abbeydorney and Lixnaw to Listowel. When he arrived, the solicitors' offices had not yet opened but his solicitude was well justified as he had the largest practice in that town.

On Monday evening we travelled by the mail train from Tralee to Killarney where the court usually sat for four days. At Farranfore junction the engine was detached in order to draw the Caherciveen goods train on to its proper track. Then it was replaced and we proceeded at a leisurely pace to Killarney. The short journey between the towns took one and a half hours during the war but we eventually arrived at the Great Southern Hotel which was, undoubtedly, the *piece de resistance* of the entire circuit.

Those who visit a great hotel today under modern conditions of travel cannot appreciate the relief which we felt when our journey from distant Listowel had ended and we entered into the civilised atmosphere of a building where the best of Victorian comforts were readily available. The long mahogany screen at the end of the classical lounge, the double flight of stairs, the large billiards room which later became the bar and the splendid dining-room that looked like the chancel of a Baroque cathedral were only part of the amenities of this fine hotel. A laundry service was provided, shoes were polished outside the door and you were wakened in the morning when Michael knocked and said: 'Sir, your bath is drawn'. The bathroom was the size of a normal bedroom in contrast to the niggardly cubicles of today and, when one returned to shave, hot water was available in a copper jug which was covered by a towel. As the war progressed we realised that such a style of living would not continue but we experienced those last few years of 'pre-war' refinement which continued until the final days of the catastrophe.

I availed of free time in the afternoons to go on rambles through the Muckross estate and along the cliff walk, or to Killeaghy graveyard (where Rudolf Erich Raspe, the original author of the *Travels and Campaigns of Baron Munchhausen*, is buried) and Lough Guitane. A favourite walk was through the Kenmare estate, with its superb oak and lime trees, and then up beyond the gardens to look at Lough Leane and Innisfallen down below with the mountains stretching from Mangerton through Purple and Tomies across to the Reeks which appeared to mingle with the sky in the distance. No attempt will be made here to discribe this wonderland which is beyond the scope of canvas or pen. If the weather is kind and when the colours are fresh or in decay no fairyland can surpass that green and lovely vale.

To stand beside the Kenmare road and look across at the Black Valley and the upper lake; to walk over Brickeen bridge and see the Eagle's Nest shimmering in a summer haze; to linger at Aghadoe and watch the whole panorama changing in colour before the twilight hour or to see swans in flight over the Laune at the castle of Dunloe was to experience many moments of unique beauty which I have filed fondly away among the archives of my memory.

Almost all the Kerry Bar assembled in Killarney. Among my deceased colleagues were Maurice Danaher, William Binchy, Tom Donovan and Billy Roche while Eoin O'Mahony and Denis Kelly usually joined us for dinner. During the war years we were often the only persons staying in the hotel especially during the spring and winter sittings. We usually sat at a large round table for our meal during which the arguments and discussions varied from history to literature and from unusual points of law to judges and politicians of former days. At that time I was mainly a silent listener and was fascinated by the knowledge and skill of my colleagues.

Eoin O'Mahony was *sui generis*. Nobody was or can be quite like him. A Corkman who had gone through two fortunes. He was often referred to as 'The Pope' because, apparently, on being asked as a schoolboy what he would like to be, he replied that he would like to be a priest because one day he might become Pope. His knowledge of local history and genealogy was so extensive and his inventive imagination so vivid that, if his memory failed in some factual details, his great flow of language continued as he clothed his stories with garments of rare texture.

He described the Habsburgs and Wittelsbachs by incidents from their family history as he likewise did of French kings and English statemen. His knowledge of Munster was particularly rich and it extended from O'Connell to de Valera and from the merchant princes of Cork to the distaff side of the landed gentry. A breath of scandal was always grist to his mill especially if his subject was a person of some historical background or social fame. A portly figure with a flat black hat and, latterly, a beard, he was always on the move and one could meet him quite unexpectedly as when I met him first on the platform at Mallow and, years later, on the platform at Harwich after his return from a clan gathering of the Butlers of Westphalia. Once on a walk along Banna strand he told me the story of Roger Casement and he confessed to me that, when he was dead, he would like his epitaph to be that he was a good Munsterman and a good European.

Denis Kelly had formerly practised on the circuit but was then retired and living in *The Hall*, Killarney. Denis was very intellectual but dogmatic and often, during an argument with Eoin, he used to say: 'The Pope is always wrong'.

When dinner was over we adjourned to the lounge for coffee and it was my duty as the junior barrister to hand around. Later Eoin had to be seen to the Imperial Hotel and Denis had to be accompanied to his home on the Cork road. At that stage Denis was often garrulous and he, almost invariably, recited the well-known stanza

36

from Swinburne!

'From too much love of living,
From hope and fear set free,
We thank with brief thanksgiving
Whatever gods may be
That no man lives forever,
That dead men rise up never;
That even the weariest river
Winds somewhere safe to sea'.

Tom Donovan was a member of an established family whose ancestral mill in Tralee bore the date 1795. Although his father had been knighted for public service in Kerry Tom had great admiration for Dr. John Charles McQuaid and Eamon de Valera from his schooldays in Blackrock College. He was State Prosecutor for Kerry and later became legal adviser to the Land Commission. Tom was always a gentleman and a loyal friend. William sometimes used to joke with him and say that, under his pretended urbanity, he was a true Kerryman as one of his eyes was brown and the other was blue!

Billy Roche's family home was at Maglass near Castleisland. His father had practised on the circuit and later became a Circuit Court judge. Billy had one of the best practices in the county particularly in Listowel and Killarney where he appeared in many important cases. He was a sound advocate and lawyer and his name appears frequently as counsel in the law reports.

Apart from the usual litigation some rather special cases were heard in Killarney from time to time. They arose from the topographical character of south Kerry. Sheep trespass and malicious injury to fisheries; ownership of a fishery by adverse possession with the accessory right of way; trespass by fire on a mountain and common of mountain grazing, with a claim for damages for over-stint, formed the subject matter of several of those cases. They were not very numerous but were more likely to occur in Killarney than elsewhere.

The courthouse had the old arrangement of seats and a convenient door opened into the Bar-room. There around the turf fire some of the best stories on the circuit were told. It was a cosy room which lent itself to conversation and the friend-liness of the solicitors added to the cosiness of the room. The yarns of Michael Casey and Jack O'Shea, of Con Healy and Michael O'Connor made the sittings memorable and, when Tom Guihan came from Kenmare, he delighted us with tales of the Lansdownes and of Sam Hussey the agent. Of the many stories which he told my favourite was the one about the Kenmare fox. It appears that some boatmen used to go from that town to a nearby island each morning and return home at night. Eventually fowl began to disappear on the island and neighbours blamed each other and the boatmen for their losses. One evening when the boat had almost reached Kenmare the engine stopped and the men began to remove some loose floor boards to reach their tool kit in the bilge of the boat. Immediately a fox jumped out from under the boards and swam home to the mainland!

A few of the more colourful cases are worth recalling. Michael Casey had a client who laid poison on his land after complying with the statutory requirements. The poison was laid at a place over twenty feet from the public road and separated from it by a thick hedge. On the other side of the road another farmer had pigs grazing on his field and some of them died after consuming portions of the poison which had, apparently, been carried across the road. Litigation ensued and Michael instructed his counsel to appear for the defendant. The case was heard in Macroom. Considerable case-law was available in old reports and, as no photostat copies of documents were then available, counsel decided to publish that law by means of an article in the law journal. On an application for a direction the cases in the article were cited in court to the chagrin of the plaintiff's solicitor who had not instructed a barrister. The direction was granted.

Another case related to the trover and conversion of turkeys on Valentia Island. It appeared that a farmer's wife had hatched a flock of turkey cocks in preparation for the Christmas market. One morning they were missing from the yard and had been replaced by turkey hens. The former were more valuable for the market. She instructed Diarmuid Rosney, her solicitor, to institute proceedings against a neighbour whom she blamed for executing the transfer. In the course of the evidence the plaintiff's husband stated that, when returning home from Mass one morning, he looked over the defendant's gate and saw his wife's turkey cocks in the yard. When asked by the judge how he knew they were his wife's turkeys he said: 'When they saw me they gobbled at me. I knew mine and they knew me'. As this was the only convincing evidence in the case the judge decided for the plaintiff and measured the damages by the difference in weight as testified by an expert witness.

Each year in March and October appeals to the High Court on Circuit were heard in Tralee. The judges then stayed in lodgings and, frequently, the most senior and most junior of the barristers were invited to dine with them. Joseph Healy S.C. almost invariably came to Tralee and, during the first inter-party government from 1948 to 1951, the late Cearbhall O'Dalaigh joined the Munster Circuit and attended regularly during the appeals.

The events which I have described briefly in this chapter came at the end of an era. The lengthy recitals and arguments to which I was a witness represented the swan song of the older

Circuit culture. There can be no Denis Kelly or Eoin O'Mahony today and no longer is there a William Binchy to recite from Marlowe's *Tamburlaine* and Carlyle's *Frederick the Great* or a Maurice Danaher to sit by the hour reading Huc's *Travels in China Tartary and Tibet*. The younger barristers are wiser in their generation than many of the men from the past. Now that society has turned full circle they appear to have taken heed of the words of scorn which Swift uttered against the inhabitants of Grub-street in his own day.

'Not Beggar's Brat, on bulk begot;
Nor Bastard of a Pedlar Scot;
Nor Boy brought up to cleaning shoes,
The Spawn of *Bridewell*, or the Stews;
Nor infants dropt, the spurious Pledges
Of *Gipsies* littering under Hedges,
Are so disqualified by Fate
To rise in *Church*, or *Law*, or *State*,
As he whom Phebus in his Ire
Hath *blasted* with poetick Fire'.

The Circuit Court in Clare

After crossing Sarsfield bridge in Limerick and having passed along the Ennis road one enters into a truly western landscape. The journey continues, beyond Woodcock Hill and beautiful Cratloe Wood, through Bunratty with its castle and folk park beside the old humpbacked Studdert Bridge. Now the estuary of the Shannon becomes visible with spectacular views of the jagged remains of Carrigogunnel and the islands and shallows of the river and further west towards distant Killadysert and Labasheeda. It is one of the noblest of prospects and a fitting prelude to this unique county of contrast and of castles. Often one saw great planes approaching the airport in later years which, in the distance, looked like giant swans descending on a lake. After Newmarket the road passes beside Dromoland Castle with its woodlands and pasture and stately demesne walls. An a hill opposite the gate-lodge a gazebo or belvedere may be seen in the form of a turret.

The castle of Clare, which was a 13th century Norman stronghold, is situated on an island of the river Fergus and it gave the name to the village of Clarecastle and to the county. After leaving Carnelly House to the left the road now approaches the village over two bridges which, up to the 1960's, were monumental humpbacked structures beside the castle and the former barracks of Clare and one got the impression, on dark winter's evenings, of approaching a medieval walled town. During the early years this road from Limerick was narrow and winding like the streets of Ennis but more recently it has been reconstructed with stone walls and attractive landscape and is as much part of a barrister's experience as the streetscape of the Circuit towns themselves.

Ennis developed in medieval days under the influence of the O'Briens whose principal seat in the 13th century was beside the ford of Clonroad. The early history of the town is closely associated with this stronghold of the Kings of Thomond and with the Franciscan Abbey or Friary which they founded in the same century. The abbey has recently been sensitively renovated as a stately ruin by the Office of Public Works but only a fragment of the later castle at Clonroad has survived in the form of a medieval doorway which had been incorporated into the wall of a 19th century residence which stands near that historic site. In later centuries Ennis was closely associated with O'Connell, Parnell and de Valera and, while the first two are commemorated today by street names, the fine O'Connell monument

dominates the square and the former Presby-
terian church has been converted into a de
Valera library and museum. His statue also
stands in the little park in front of the courthouse.

Ennis is the most charming town on the
Circuit and one of the most attractive in the
country. The Fergus meanders through it on its
journey to the Shannon and the sea. When in
flood it hurries along silently in a dignified and
placid manner behind the backs of houses and
under the single-span stone bridge near the
abbey after which it proceeds onwards between
Steele's rock and the lime trees and buildings of
18th century Abbeyfield House. There it sweeps
to the right and continues onwards towards
Clarecastle and the estuary.

The barristers usually stayed at Carmody's
Hotel which stood almost opposite the abbey. It
was an ancient tumbledown house when I commenced practising on the Circuit during the war.
With its corridors and dark rooms, which had
frosted glass in the windows, one often got the
impression of living underground but the
annexe, to which it was connected by an over-
head passage, had some spacious rooms with
thick walls and shutters. This annexe is still part
of an attractive terrace of houses although the
main buildings of the hotel have been
demolished.

In those early years the lists were light and the

court rarely sat for the whole of the second week during the term. The usual types of civil cases differed but little from those in Kerry or Limerick. Applications under the Landlord and Tenant and the Rent Restrictions Act were common as were District Court appeals and cases dealing with negligence, trespass, ejectment and breaches of warranty. Actions relating to easements of rights of way were met with as frequently as in Kerry while applications for workmen's compensation and compensation for malicious damages to property were rarely absent. In these latter applications the knocking of stone walls around farms was sometimes the gist of the complaint. Ennis had its share of equity suits while applications for title to registered land by adverse possession were numerous in Clare but for convenience these land registry applications were usually brought in Dublin. In later years an interesting case relating to the right to take seaweed from the foreshore was heard in Kilrush and, on appeal, at the High Court on Circuit in Ennis and in a case where the plaintiff's animal had strayed into the graveyard at Quin Abbey and died after eating the foliage of a yew tree the plaintiff succeeded against the county council on whom lay the duty to maintain the graveyard. The seven streams of the Burren featured in a Circuit Court action while, in recent times, the question of a public charitable trust relating to the grant of a perpetual supply of free water to the inhabitants of certain townlands in the Burren was questioned by the county council under legislation relating to water charges.

Clare has some of the most melodious place-names in Ireland which became familiar from maps or documents of title. One came across such names as Ballinalacken, Ballynacally, Bodyke, Buncraggy, Ballyalla, Cratloekeel, Crusheen and Corkscrew Hill as well as Drumcliffe, Kilkishen, Spancil Hill, Labasheeda, Islandmagrath, Dysert O'Dea, Spanish Point, Paulnasherry, Kilfenora, O'Callaghan's Mills, Mauricesmills and sweet Corofin. In my memory, however, the most delightful combination of place names arose in a land case in which the property was described in the brief as being situated in Islandavanna Upper and Islandavanna Lower in the Barony of Islands and County of Clare.

One of the main attractions of Ennis arises from the quality and lay-out of the streets. The principal streets are particularly narrow and they converge at O'Connell Square while Bank Place, Bindon Street and Harmony Row form a kind of later residential or suburban development. The *ensemble* is quite delightful and the fine character of the buildings and shops, with here and there a handful of archaic and even quaint structures, gives the town an alluring personality which, in the main, time has neither ravaged nor destroyed but only caressed. Several of the Russell and Bannatyne corn stores or mills may still be seen on the outskirts but one regrets the loss of River View House and the old mill beside the weir.

A walk from the Old Ground Hotel brings one through the heart of the town and then along by the river until the courthouse is reached. This is a splendid Palladian building on a hill with a spacious hall which contains a monument to Sir Michael O'Loghlen Bart, the Master of the Rolls. It is the most elegant courthouse on the Circuit and the courtrooms are in the old style with the barristers' seats near the judge and the witness. Each room contains a balcony appropriately curved in sympathy with the internal design. A wide corridor runs outside at the back of each court and this facilitates consultations and discussions. It is unlikely to be changed because the design and construction of the building were sensitively conceived and executed.

The *camaraderie* on the Clare Circuit was never as clearly apparent as in Limerick or Kerry. While a Bar-room was provided in the annexe to Carmody's it was never as popular a *rendezvous* as its counterpart in the other counties. The real meeting place in Ennis was the cosy little bar in the hotel which the solicitors and barristers frequented or the small corridor beside the principal courtroom where a peep-window enabled the proceedings to be followed.

In those early years, at least, the quantity of work was less in Clare than elsewhere on the

Circuit. William Binchy, William Roche and Tom Donovan never practised there while Paddy Griffin, the State Prosecutor, lived in the country. George Kenny frequently stayed at Carmody's although his home was at Freagh Castle near Miltown Malbay until the death of his parents. Owen Keane, who has recently retired from practice, stayed in the family residence at *Hermitage* near Ennis. Later George made the Queens Hotel his permanent home and Maurice Danaher joined him there during the sittings. George never practised outside Clare and Limerick in my experience and he rarely, if ever, went to Dublin. Eventually Maurice and George retired to Carrigoran nursing home near Newmarket where, advanced in years, they died within a few months of each other in 1980.

The remainder of the barristers usually went to the Old Ground Hotel in later years and I can recall holding many consultations there, after the evening journey from Dublin, under a print of Derrynane Abbey while enjoying tea and sandwiches during the discussions. These were interesting country cases in which I was briefed by John Casey or Niall Casey and they eventually comprised the bulk of my Clare practice.

A popular short walk after dinner was over the bridges at Bank Place and Abbey Street and, in the afternoons, if the work was slack, a walk by the railway line to Clare Abbey was a rewarding experience especially in spring when one often heard the cuckoo calling from a nearby crag. The abbey is situated on a mound or hillock and, stretching away in front, is a broad area of marsh or fen land so characteristic of parts of the county. The site of the abbey together with this marshy plain were probably intended as a physical protection for the monks in this antique landscape which appeared to have changed but little over the centuries.

On a few occasions trips were made to the Burren to see the great limestone plateau and the beautiful gentian flowers or to Corcomroe Abbey or Quin, and to Leamaneh Castle or the cliffs of Moher to watch heavy seas running in Liscannor Bay. In later years visits were made to Bunratty and Craggaunowen.

During my early years at the Bar certain tenuous links still existed with the Old Munster Circuit of the turn of the century. Edward (Ned) McElligott, who was a native of Listowel, had been Crown Prosecutor for Cork city before his appointment as Judge of the South Western Circuit. Years later, when he had retired, I was introduced to him in Ballybunnion by William Binchy and, when Judge O'Briain sat in Listowel for the first time, Judge McElligott sat with him on the bench briefly for the purpose of welcoming him to the town. After his retirement he gave a farewell dinner at the Dolphin Hotel in Dublin. I remember that evening well in the old Edwardian hostelry near the river with its atmosphere of the past and with quatrains from Omar Khayyám spreading across the walls. It was an historic occasion with several nostalgic speeches which were in effect the swan-song of an era that was passing away under the pressures of the war. Not long afterwards we attended his Requiem Mass in Phibsboro. George Kenny's father was Matthew Kenny who had been a member of parliament and then Crown Prosecutor for Kerry before being appointed Judge of the Southern Circuit in Cork. On his retirement he lived in the old home at Freagh until his death. John A. Costello, who became Attorney General, one of the leaders of the Bar and Taoiseach, had practised in Clare for seven years.

Among the local members of the older Circuit were Patrick Lynch, Michael Comyn and James Comyn. Patrick Lynch was eventually appointed Attorney General by Eamon de Valera against whom he had stood in the East Clare by-election in 1917 and Michael Comyn became Judge of the Eastern Circuit. It was his brother James who signed my memorial when I enrolled as a student at King's Inns. The Comyn family came from Ballyvaughan and, in a lease of 1877, which was an exhibit in a recent case in Ennis, a James Comyn was a signatory as one of the guardians of the Ballyvaughan Union. Michael Comyn was also the owner of phosphate mines in Doolin. I can recall a historic dinner which he gave in

Lisdoonvarna to which he invited the judge, barristers and solicitors and the local clergy. It was perhaps the last of the patriarchal dinners on the Circuit. These old retired judges were steeped in the common law and equity. The procedure had changed but little in their time and statute law was largely confined to aspects of malicious injury and land cases while text-books were traditional and well annotated by the practitioners. It was fashionable at Bar dinners for speakers to bemoan the absence of up-to-date Irish text-books but now, in the fullness of fashion, these have become as thick as autumnal leaves.

Happy memories of the Circuit are associated with occasional visits to Carnelly House which was the home of Dr. Dermot F. Gleeson District Justice and author of *A History of the Diocese of Killaloe* and of other books on aspects of the local history Ormond. Carnelly was the birth place of Lord O'Brien of Kilfenora — better known as Peter the Packer — and the stately avenue, which is shaded by many mature trees, is said to be haunted by the ghost of Maura Rua of Leamaneh Castle. One evening after tea Dr. Gleeson showed some drafts and proofs of the history to Dermot Kinlen and myself after which we adjourned to the beautiful drawing-room with its rich plasterwork to enjoy an evening's conversation around the fire. It was a journey into the past as though the violence of the 20th century was but a sordid episode from a Gothic novel. Pleasant evenings were also spent with that great gentleman, Michael McMahon of Kilrush, the *doyen* of the Clare solicitors, in his old-world home in Kilkee or with Flan and Carmel O'Reilly in Ennis while Michael Nolan of Kilkee, who loved the open air, took one on trips to Carriga-holt and Loop Head to see the lighthouse and get magnificent views of the great estuary and the Atlantic.

Once each term we went to Kilrush for a day leaving Ennis early for the long journey which was often bleak and lonely in winter. There the list was usually light and sometimes the court had finished by lunch time. The courthouse had been erected in 1831 and was the most archaic on the Circuit. It had been built flush with the street, and one entered by an archway into an outer hall paved with flagstones which had be-come smooth from the boots of countless litigants and witnesses. It was there that consultations were held and settlements negotiated. The court-room had the older form of seating and at the back was a balcony from which locals sometimes watched the proceedings. The ivy, which had accumulated on the windowsills and around the frames, became agitated on windy days and this added to the atmosphere of a genuine country courthouse. The Bar-room was upstairs and had windows looking out on to the woods of the former Vandeleur demesne with the Protestant church and a family monument or mausoleum clearly visible. It had solid wooden chairs, an old wooden table, a bare deal floor and a press filled with bound volumes of Victorian and later statutes. It was also the last Bar-room on the Circuit to retain the turf fire. I can recall a day in the early 1980's piling on turf and holding a consultation beside the fire with Michael McMahon who had retired as a solicitor but was an essential witness in a probate action listed for hearing before Judge Desmond that day. When the court had risen the old courthouse keeper used to stand at the door and bid us farewell. Everything about Kilrush court was traditional!

Kilrush is essentially an 18th and 19th century market town which has changed but little over the years and some of the old stone pavements and shop fronts have survived. Frances street, which sweeps down to the water, is one of the widest in the land and, at the top of the street near the market house, is the monument to the Manchester Martyres with inscriptions in French, Irish and English engraved on it. The fine stone buildings of the Catholic church and the convent add to the character of the town as do the surviving old grain stores and the grand facility of Cappa pier. If we had to remain overnight in Kilrush we stayed at Williams's Hotel and took a walk around the town or to Cappa with the view beyond to historic Scattery Island (Inis Cathaigh). On rare occasions we were able to spend an evening and night in Kilkee in the summer but the usual procedure was that we had lunch in the hotel and went back quickly to Ennis when the court had risen.

There were of course, moments of humour and even drama in the court and memorable evenings were passed in Carmody's cosy bar with the older colleagues holding the floor but these were ephemeral occasions in which the humour was more suitable for the spoken than the written word. In this chapter I have refrained from repeating Circuit stories which have already been published and have reduced to a minimum any reference to my deceased colleagues as they have been sufficiently described in the Limerick and Kerry chapters.

In the absence of records the past is irretrievably lost except to the memory which itself often becomes clouded and by its nature is selective. I have kept no diary and did not have the help of any documents apart from a few law reports and some topographical and literary material when writing this memoir of the South Western Circuit for the years after 1942. The only excuse which can be offered for this inadequate presentation is that half of the loaf is better than no bread when recalling the daily round of those whom James Meagher, the Mitchelstown barrister, had described, in relation to the old Circuit, as 'the gallant bands of brothers who with light pockets and high hopes took, twice a year, the road from Ennis to Cork'. And perhaps it is fitting that I should conclude with a citation from a masterly review of Maurice Healy's *Old Munster Circuit* which Jim Meagher had published in *The Clongownian* in 1939:

Names are we, and voices only, passing on our little round,

Words that perish all our labour, all our toil an empty sound.

In the dark and hurrying future, the inheritors of life,

Outstretched hands, uplifted faces, wait their summons to the strife.

They shall wake the solemn echoes, they shall tread the ancient street,

Hastening from court to lodging — fresher voices, younger feet.

Then our boyhood's labours ended, ended then our manhood's boasts,

Shadows whispering from somewhere, We shall be the circuit ghosts!